> **Teachers are spec...**
>
> **They affect**
>
> **our lives**
>
> **forever,**
>
> **in many special ways.**

To contact Gail Kervatt

gkervatt@gmail.com

PO Box 2323

Oak Ridge, NJ 07438

www.selective-mutism.com

Table of Contents

Preface

Selective mutism is a complex psychological disorder with an unknown origin. It is one of the most misdiagnosed anxiety disorders in the world. Recent studies state that selective mutism may occur in .7 to 2% of early elementary students, although many researchers agree that these prevalence rates may be underrepresented due to the lack of knowledge and diagnosis of the disorder (Cunningham, McHolm, & Boyle, 2006; Lescano, 2008; Schwartz et al., 2006; Sharkey, McNicholas, Barry, Begley, & Ahern, 2007). Generally, selective mutism is called shyness for several years until a child enters school and does not function verbally in school and most social situations outside of school. Parents and teachers become very concerned and seek further assistance and diagnosis. These children have the ability to speak and understand language, develop age appropriate skills, and function normally at home and with most family members. However, if the behavior last for a period of time, it becomes a learned pattern and is difficult to overcome because, the longer a child is silent, the more entrenched the behavior becomes.

Most School personnel do not have the experience or expertise to accommodate a child having this psychological disorder which is caused by anxiety and avoidance. The numbers of children identified who are suffering with selective mutism have risen sharply in the past few years. A letter from a parent asking for help was published in a parenting magazine a few years ago, along with some television segments and news articles and many cases have since surfaced. The school system in which I work now has one child in first grade and two children in kindergarten who have been identified as having selective mutism, which makes four children within five years in one small suburban school system.

Many medical personnel are, also, not aware of the disorder or they have found that traditional psychotherapy has been disappointing. Michelle Cottle (*The New Republic*, August 2, 1999) reports that research indicates one in every eight persons may have a social phobia and even though pharmacological intervention is widely advocated, the relapse rate is 50 percent within six months of stopping medication.

It is my purpose in the book to present a case history and to describe my experience as an elementary school reading specialist with a selectively mute child. Also described is the process

that followed in his overcoming the disorder after five years of being mute in school and all social situations. I do not guarantee that these activities will work with all children or any other child as there are many variables, but would hope that if the information could be of help to one parent, child or teacher, my goal would be accomplished.

Chapter One

History

"There's a boy who doesn't talk." The classroom kindergarten teacher made the statement in a casual manner. The statement, as was told to me, was quite disconcerting, as my job as an elementary school reading specialist is to test the children within the school at various times throughout the year in order to check their reading progress and place them in instructional reading groups for the following year. The Anton Brenner Test had been administered in the kindergarten classroom to do some initial screening in October. The test identifies children who may have a weakness in language development. How was it possible that Nicholas had not been noticed by the responsible administering faculty? Why had there been no earlier notification of Nicholas' lack of speech? The screening test is a nonverbal test in which the children copy a series of dots and then a sentence. Next, they draw a man and then count pictures of objects. The entire group screening is written. Therefore, the children do not need to speak and Nicholas scored quite high. He was not identified as needing any type of accommodations or intervention.

It was now June. The Slosson Test of Reading Readiness, an instrument requiring expressive language, had to be administered to Nicholas in order to make a reading group placement for the first grade. A meeting had to be arranged with the kindergarten classroom teacher, Nicholas' mother and me to discuss an approach to this quandary.

The history revealed that Nicholas had been in preschool for three years due to the fact that his birthday is in November. He had stopped speaking in preschool at the end of his first year in a four year old class. The lack of speech was attributed to a death in the family of an uncle and possibly to pressure put on him to speak by a teacher at summer camp. Nicholas would only speak in his home to his mother, father, younger brother and a few relatives, and even there, he was extremely selective with whom he would speak. He would speak to an uncle who lived halfway across the country and occasionally visited, but he would not speak to an uncle and cousins who lived close and visited frequently.

During his kindergarten year, Nicholas would occasionally whisper to one schoolmate who was a close friend in preschool, but in a secretive manner. Nicholas' parents were becoming, understandably, quite concerned about his learning and functioning both at school and

at home. It was reported by his mother that their pediatrician had assured them that Nicholas would "outgrow" his shyness.

Nicholas had met with our speech and language pathologist, a member of the Special Services Department, midyear of his kindergarten year, as did all kindergarten children, to be screened for language difficulties. Nicholas had been told by his mother earlier that if he would say one word to the teacher during this screening, he could go to the local toy store and buy any toy of his choosing. Still, Nicholas would not speak and was not identified as a speech candidate, because no articulation problems were evident due to the fact that he wouldn't speak. The suggested approach to the kindergarten teacher and parent by the speech and language pathologist and the school psychologist was to let Nicholas enjoy his kindergarten year, to enjoy the teacher whom he loved and to see what would happen.

Nicholas had not spoken in school for two years by the end of kindergarten. He would not use the school toilet. He would not even laugh out loud. He displayed all the characteristics of any six year old child: happy, eager to learn, participating in all activities as long as he could be silent. Often, the class would develop chart stories, each child adding a sentence to be written by the teacher. Nicholas was so eager to participate that he began bringing sentences written at home to add to the stories. He would point to objects in the classroom to answer questions. The teacher continued to treat and talk to Nicholas as she would any other child in the class. His ideas were being conveyed as he learned to use avoidance techniques in the school environment to accommodate his disability.

Nicholas was informed by his mother in June of his kindergarten year that he would have to take the Slosson Test and would have to respond orally by saying one word answers. He agreed to come to the testing situation with his mother at his side. The first section or the test involves naming upper and lower case letters. Nicholas whispered the responses to his mother and she relayed them to me. He scored quite well.

He had to state rhyming words for the next section of the screening, at which time his voice became an audible whisper as he became more comfortable and confident with the testing situation. His mother informed him that she couldn't hear him, so as to get him to speak louder. At one point, as he was whispering to her that she had stated the wrong answer, I replied to her that it was sufficient because I could hear him. Nicholas' face became ashen and for a moment it appeared that he might run from the room. The seriousness of this disorder of which I knew

little suddenly became quite evident to me, and Nicholas' reaction indicated that this disability would probably not be easily overcome. Research, on my part, definitely had to be pursued. This beautiful little boy was obviously bright, but how would he learn to read, comprehend and function within his first grade classroom?

September came and Nicholas was now in first grade. He was placed in the high group for his reading instruction. A conference with the new classroom teacher, parent, principal and me was arranged in October so that we could obtain some more history and develop a plan to help Nicholas overcome his fears and learn to read. Nicholas had begun to see a PH.D. candidate in psychology on a weekly basis outside of the school setting. She diagnosed him as "selectively mute" and her input was used to devise some beginning goals for Nicholas. The goals were as follows:

- The classroom teacher and Nicholas' mom would explain selective mutism to the class and, at another time, to the faculty.
- Nicholas would be encouraged to mouth words at the reading table or mouth poems in the classroom library.
- The entire class would mouth words or poems together.
- He would be encouraged to whisper to the classroom teacher.
- His mom would invite friends from the classroom for play dates at his house. (The first child was to be the one child to whom Nicholas had continued whispering in preschool.)
- The classroom teacher would invite Nicholas' mom to school to talk for him when it was his turn to be Star Student. (Each week, a bulletin board would be devoted to one child on which to place pictures and artifacts about themselves, then orally share with the class as Star Student).
- His mom would invite the kindergarten and first grade teachers to Nicholas' house to visit after school
- The first grade teacher would encourage Nicholas to use the kindergarten bathroom, which was more private, when the need was presented.

Through his weekly therapy sessions with the outside psychologist, Nicholas' mom had by now become more aware of the seriousness of selective mutism. She had pursued some research on her own through The Selective Mutism Foundation and made that information available to the

classroom teacher and me. Even though Nicholas' mom was quite nervous herself about speaking in front of a group, she delivered a very informative presentation to the faculty explaining the term "Selective Mutism". She completed her presentation by showing a video of Nicholas in his home. It showed a vivacious, witty and talkative little boy. The information she presented was practical and enlightening to the faculty, as none of the teachers had ever faced this situation with a student and their educational responses and recommendations regarding Nicholas had been quite varied. Nicholas had become known to the faculty as, "the boy who doesn't talk" and their fears of having him as a student and not knowing how to help him had become extremely evident.

Within the classroom, the teacher explained Nicholas' behavior to the children. She explained it as a shyness and let them know that when, and if, Nicholas ever spoke, they should not overreact to it. The children were openly responsive to the suggestions and included him in all of their group activities. They spoke to him, even though they knew he would probably not verbally respond back. Nicholas continued to point to answers and use hand gestures and facial expressions to communicate with the children; so, they treated him as any other classmate, but one who wouldn't speak. They included him in all of their activities, both in the classroom and on the playground where he ran and played as arduously as all the other children.

During this first grade year, most of the established goals were not accomplished. Nicholas would not mouth words or whisper to the classroom teacher. The friends' home visits went well, however, Nicholas would only speak to his past friend from preschool when he thought no one, including his mother, would see or hear him. His mother came to school for the Star Student presentation and did the speaking for Nicholas. He enjoyed this experience and participated in every way except verbally, feeling confident that he, again, could remain silent.

One or two days a week, Nicholas stayed after school with his mother and preschool brother to develop a rapport with the classroom teacher. The extended day was coordinated with his weekly appointments with the psychologist. After many months of this arrangement, Nicholas would occasionally whisper to his mother to communicate his wants to the classroom teacher, especially if he wanted to use the computer.

Toward the end of the year, the classroom teacher visited Nicholas' home to further develop a rapport with him. He was pleased that she came to visit, but he did not speak. Later in

the year, Nick's mother bought a toy that he undoubtedly desired. She gave it to the classroom teacher to offer to Nick after school one day, as an incentive for Nick to say, "Thank you." He wanted the toy so much that he reluctantly made an extremely garbled guttural "sound" to say, "Thank you." Did this mean that material incentives could be used to break through the barrier? Possibly, this was a strategy that could now be used to encourage verbalization.

The only other speaking goal Nicholas accomplished toward the end of first grade was that he made a burping sound. Soon afterward, he attended a classmate's birthday party and was quite proud to burp at people. Nicholas has a witty sense of humor and appeared to enjoy seeing the reaction of both adults and children when he would make the burping sound. His actions were the beginning of verbalizing in front of other people. He was testing his actions against their reactions.

Another goal to be accomplished in first grade was for Nick to learn to read. Our school reading program is based on Continuous Progress levels. The levels range from 1 to 15 and encompass Grades 1 through 5. Nicholas would be required to learn the skills on levels 1 through 7 to complete the standard first grade reading curriculum. The skills included phonics, sight words, comprehension, study skills and literature appreciation. In order to facilitate his reading another conference was arranged with Nick's mother to discuss home instruction and to provide the appropriate level sheet and materials. She readily agreed to use the materials, which included a phonics workbook, a basal reader and a workbook. Suggested methods were to be used to help him learn to read.

A reading group would gather in the classroom each day and Nick was included in the small group instruction. He would read silently and listen to all instruction, participating only nonverbally. Much group work was done on a classroom rug, where Nicholas was encouraged to mouth words to poems or predictable stories. However, he refused to do so, and no verbal progress was made.

Nicholas's writing skills also appeared to be weak at this time, especially in the area of details and expanding upon a topic. He would write one word or one sentence to complete journal entries or writing assignments and had to be coaxed to complete the minimum. His fear of communicating was now overflowing into his ability to convey ideas in the written form.

In spite of all of this, apparently Nicholas, being quite bright and observant, had absorbed most concepts presented during his first grade year. All first grade children were tested in January, using a standard word recognition test. Nicholas agreed to record the word lists at home and scored a Preprimer III word recognition level, which was an appropriate level for the middle of first grade. This was a big step for Nick, to record the words and let his voice be heard by a teacher. He would not allow me to listen to the tape recording in his presence. However, he was allowing his voice to be heard by another person, even if she was one that he had not selected.

June came and again all of the children were tested. Nicholas once more made his recording at home, but easily read the provided words. He brought the recording to my classroom and waited outside the door while I listened. He would not yet allow anyone to listen to his voice in his presence. Upon reviewing the recording, it was obvious that the words were too easy and Nick needed to read more words at a higher level so that his present word recognition level could be determined. The end of the year was fast approaching and class groupings were being prepared for the next year. There was no time left. Nicholas was asked to go into the small book room next door to read and record as many words as he could. Of course, he was reluctant to do this, but he was assured that he would be alone, the room was soundproof and the door would be closed so that no one could hear him.

Nick complied with the request and recorded the words. His voice sounded at ease, even though he spoke very softly. He became rather witty at one point. While reading fourth grade level words, he stated, "I don't know what these words mean, but I guess I'm supposed to read them!" Nick tested at the end of third grade level in word recognition. More importantly, he had produced his voice at school, knowing that another person would be listening to it. We had moved from a burp to his voice being produced and heard in the school setting. This was one small step, but a very important step.

In addition to recording the word lists, Nicholas' mother administered an individual reading inventory to him at home. His reading and responses were recorded. Nick read two difficult second grade reading selections aloud and answered all of the comprehension questions correctly. He could now read and he actually read above grade level. He was ready for second grade, but he was still silent in the school and all settings outside of his home.

The bookroom recording incident became a catalyst for using another recording for the children who were to be in Nicholas' class the following year to hear his voice on the first day of the new school year. Nick's biggest fear was that if he spoke at school, the other children would laugh at his voice. He had told his mom that he felt his voice sounded "funny".

It was now the last day of first grade and after conferring with the psychologist, the new teacher and the parent, each child who was to be in Nicholas' second grade class was called to my room separately, including Nicholas, to record one page of a story about friends. The children involved in the reading would not be identified on the recording. Neither were they told of the intended purpose of the recording, although Nick appeared to sense that it was somehow connected to his lack of speech. The recording would be played in Nick's class the first day of second grade after summer break. The class would view the big book from which the text was taken while listening to the recording. The listening activity would be an introduction to the theme of "Friends". The second grade teacher had been carefully chosen for Nick, as well as the children to be included in his class. Two of the children, whom we believed to whom Nicholas whispered secretly, were placed in his class along with other children and a teacher who would accept his disorder, would be willing to be kind and, most of all, patient with him.

Chapter Two
Research

Two days of school remained for the faculty members. Several hours were spent on the Internet searching for some information about selective mutism. Little information about selective mutism was available at this time, however, The Low Incident Support Center in Australia supplied a listing of articles that had been published on the subject of selective mutism and interventions within a school setting. Although dated now, these articles are very specific to the school setting and selective mutism, a rare find, and are still very applicable. The list was faxed to our high school librarian who agreed to see if she could obtain the articles through the county inter-library loan service since the articles that can be referenced on the Internet are usually abstracts or summaries. Our librarian was able to get full copies of four of the twenty articles from my list. Although there is much more research available today, the following is a listing of those articles and a chapter from a text found to be exceptionally helpful in developing behavioral techniques. The five very useful resources used for my school intervention are as follows:

- Brown, B. & Doll, B. (1988) *Case Illustration of Classroom Intervention with an Elective Mute Child, Special Services in the Schools,* 5 (1/2), 107-125.
- Giddan, Jane J.; Ross, Gloria J.; Sechler, Linda L. Becker, Bonnetta R. (1977) *Schools, Selective Mutism in Elementary School : Multidisciplinary Interventions, Language, Speech and Hearing Services in the School,* 28, 127-133.
- Kehle, Thomas J., Hintze, John M., DuPaul, George J. (1997). *Selective Mutism.* In T. Alex, G. Bear, and K. Minke (Eds.), *Children's Needs II: Development, Problems and Alternatives,* (pp. 329-337). *National Association of School Psychologists.*
- Lazarus, P., Gavello, H., Moore, J. (1983) *The Treatment of Elective Mutism in Children Within the School Setting: Two Case Studies, School Psychology Review,* 12(4), 467-472.
- Richburg, M.L., & Cobia, D. (1994) *Using Behavioral Techniques to Treat Elective Mutism: A Case Study. Elementary School Guidance & Counseling,* 28, 214-219.

Two other Internet sites were found from which to access information on selective mutism. The Selective Mutism Group (www.selectivemutism.org) has a wealth of information, services and support. Included on the website are lists of treating professionals and support groups around the world. The Selective Mutism Foundation (www.selectivemutismfoundation.org), founded by two parents of selectively mute children, also, contains much information on selective mutism.

Chapter Three
Changing Gears

After an investigation of the research, my return to school the following September was with the firm conviction that a systematic behavioral intervention was necessary, as was employing the appropriate school personnel. Someone had to begin to take responsibility for providing Nicholas with the type of school setting and accommodations he needed to help overcome, or at least improve, his verbalizations.

A review of the case studies about selective mutism surfaced several important points:

- The longer selective mutism persists, the more debilitating it becomes (Kehle, Hintze, & DuPaul, 1997; Giddan, Ross, Sechler, & Becker, 1997).

- Selective mutism is a very complex anxiety disorder. (Brown & Doll, 1998).

- Interventions ideally require collaboration between the school psychologist and/or speech and language pathologist and the home (Kehle, Hintze, & DuPaul, 1997; Richburg & Cobia, 1994; Lazarus, Gavilo, & Moore, 1993; Geddan, Ross, Sechler, & Becker, 1997).

- Interventions shown to be most effective have employed behavior therapy approaches including contingency management, stimulus fading, escape or avoidance techniques, self-modeling, positive reinforcement and pharmacological treatment. Effective treatment studies incorporated a combination of behavioral techniques (Kehle, Hintze, & DuPaul, 1997; Richburg & Cobia, 1994; Lazarus, Gavilo, & Moore, 1983).

- Stimulus fading involves the gradual fading of settings and other individuals such as the teacher and classmates into the child's normal verbal interactions (Kehle, Hintze, & DuPaul, 1997).

- It is more efficient to first shape audible speech in a controlled environment using systematic desensitization techniques to address the phobic anxiety, than to employ a whole-class procedure to encourage speech. The case study child was gradually pulled into group situations, required to participate in classroom activities and allowed to become accustomed to the experience of being in a group (Brown & Doll, 1988).

- Strategies and reinforcers might include task requirements, recordings, puppets, animal sounds, games, whispering, a classroom pet, prizes, bubble blowers, telephones, pantomime and masks (Lazarus, Gavilo, & Moore, 1983; Giddan, Ross, Sechler, & Becker, 1997).
- Once the child begins speaking in the school setting, it is important to expand the speaking to the home setting, community settings and other relatives (Giddan, Ross, Sechler, & Becker, 1997).

Another discussion to resolve the issue was scheduled which included the principal, guidance counselor, speech pathologist and me. The research findings were discussed along with a plea for some intervention by the responsible parties. The replies were, "It's not a speech problem." and "I would not feel comfortable or competent working with this child." It appeared that in order for Nicholas to receive any help at school, the onus was to fall on me. This was not my area of expertise, certification or experience. However, someone had to make an effort to help this child. Three periods a week, in my already crowded schedule, were set aside to try to provide Nicholas with appropriate accommodations.

The next arranged meeting included the principal, Special Services school psychologist and me. It was my feeling that this situation was a Section 504 of the Rehabilitation Act of 1973. Section 504 protects qualified individuals with disabilities. Under this law, individuals with disabilities are defined as persons with a physical or mental impairment which substantially limits one or more major life activities. People who have a history of, or who are regarded as having a physical or mental impairment that substantially limits one or more major life activities, are also covered. Major life activities include caring for one's self, walking, seeing, hearing, speaking, breathing, working, performing manual tasks, and learning. The only assistance offered, however, was a weekly check of my intervention in cooperation with the classroom teacher by the school psychologist.

The place to start would be with recordings since Nick was already familiar with this type of verbalization. He had recorded word lists and pages of a book in first grade. By now, the class had heard his recorded voice reading from a book on the first day of school. Nicholas' response was not terribly positive to the class playback, as he later reiterated to his mother, but

he realized that no one laughed upon hearing his anonymous voice. One major fear had already been reduced.

Nick's mother, psychologist and classroom teacher advised him that this year in second grade he would be responsible for completing tasks to work toward overcoming his fears and he would be receiving help at school three times a week. They devised a list of monetary incentives to encourage his classroom attempts to speak. Some of these task were to be completed during his three additional special classes and some were to be attempted within the classroom. Another list of goals was developed, with Nicholas' input, to be documented weekly during his three individual and small group sessions. Nick continued to see the private psychologist on a weekly basis, working toward attempts to verbalize with her.

The pages that follow are the actual notes written following each of Nick's three scheduled periods with me. They include Nick's handwritten goal for each week along with any forms that were devised. The classes, covering almost a full academic year, began in late October and continued through mid May.

The chronology of the weekly goal sheets points out that Nicholas began speaking in a gruff "throat" voice in the spring of second grade. He began speaking in a normal voice shortly after school was dismissed for the summer vacation and he continues to do so in all social settings to this day. Medication was never used, much to Nick's parents' relief. Even though it took almost a full calendar year to achieve these outcomes, Nicholas is now an active and eager participating member of his total social environment.

Chapter Four
Descriptions of Classes, Strategies and Activities

Second Grade Psychologist Prepared Classroom Incentive Chart

NICHOLAS

1¢	Make a tape. Make a noise when you answer a question in class.
5¢	Whisper an answer to John.
10¢	Make a tape when someone else is in the room with you. Mouth a word in class.
20¢	Whisper to Michael.
25¢	ana n l sounds
50¢	Whisper to Miss Ciarlo. Whisper to Mrs. Karvatt.
$1.00	Say one word out loud in class.

PRIZE #1: 10¢ FOR CANDY EVERY DAY

PRIZE #2:

Nicholas

Goals for Communication
October

Stories will be recorded for the classroom with Mrs. Kervatt or Mom. Each child in the class will record one line, including Nick, to be used as a listening center, played as part of a classroom theme study.
Dates 9/3, 9/15, 9/19, 10/6, 10/2, 10/10, 10/24, 11/15, 12/2

Class with Mrs. Kervatt three times a week to record animal sounds on the computer using Scholastic, *Wiggle Works* computer program. Listen with a partner and Mrs. Kervatt.
Dates 10/15, 10/20, 10/28, 11/19, 12/11

Make animal sounds.
Dates 11/11, 11/17, 11/19, 11/26, 11/27, 12/3, 12/4, 12/9, 12/10, 12/11, 12/17, 12/18, 12/23, 1/8,

Play board games using two voice recorders to answer Yes or No questions.
Dates 10/28, 11/3

Mouth "Yes" or "No to answer board game questions.
Dates 11/4, 11/4, 11/10, 11/11, 11/17 (red), 11/20 (animal sounds), 11/24, 1/5

Use puppets to make animal sounds.
Dates 11/26, 12/3, 12/10, 12/17, 12/23

Record a speaking prompt to be played in the classroom.
Dates 12/11

Whisper "Yes" or "No" to answer board game questions.
Dates

Record with Mrs. Kervatt outside the slightly open door.
Dates

Record with Mrs. Kervatt or friend in the room.
Dates

Use message recorders to answer "Yes" or "No" questions in the classroom.
Dates

 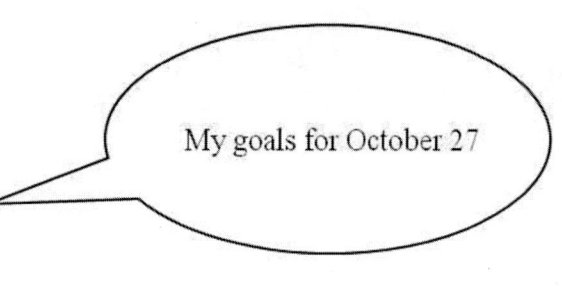

My goals for October 27

Class #1:

1. Nicholas was provided a journal in which to respond to prewritten questions. Question #1 Tell me why you find it hard to get the words out at school? His written response was: I am shy. Question #2 What are your fears? His response was, "People might be shouting and screaming." Question #3 What do you want to happen when you are able to speak? His response was, "Not yelling and screaming."
2. Nick tape recorded on the computer five pages of a Scholastic, *Wiggle Works* story about a bear and a mouse. Nick's friend, Michael, came to class with Nick and recorded the mouse part of the story on every other page, alternating with Nick. We had to stay outside the door while Nick did his recording.
3. Nick made a bear sound on the recording at the end of each of the bear's dialog.
4. Nick brought his rock collection to share with me.
5. Nick borrowed an electronic game to take home as a prize for the sounds he made.

Class #2:

1. Nick brought his friend John to class. John is the one child from preschool with whom Nick continued to secretly speak in a whisper at school.
2. Nick finished his classroom spelling sent up by his classroom teacher.
3. He was then instructed to record "Yes" and "No" into a message recorder. He did so while in the room with John. I had to wait outside the door.
4. The two boys played the game "Language Trivia". I asked only "yes" and "no" questions. Nick would answer using his voice recorder. He became comfortable with this knowing that I had previously listened to his recorded voice.

Class #3:

Nick was absent.

My goal for October 27th

making more taps

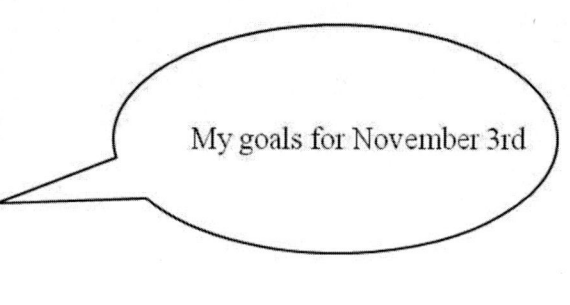

My goals for November 3rd

Class #1:

Election Day

Class #2

1. We played "Language Trivia" again with John. Nicholas used his message recorder to answer "Yes" and mouthed the word "No" three times.
2. Nick's prize was a piece of Franklinite mineral. John and Nick spent five minutes looking at it glow under a black light

Class #3

1. Nicholas and Michael were given journals again and asked to respond to a prompt. Nick's prompt was, List four reasons why it would be helpful to speak at school. His responses were, 1. "I could answer easier." 2. "I could talk to my friends." 3. "I could talk things out." 4. "I could answer questions." Michael, also, wrote reasons why it would be helpful for Nick to speak at school. He read his responses to Nick. Nick preferred that I read his responses aloud to Michael. The boys seemed to have a common bond of wanting very badly to communicate with each other.
2. We played "Language Trivia" again to communicate with "Yes" and "No" questions. Nick mouthed the words voluntarily. He indicated by pointing that he would like another Franklinite rock as a prize. We agreed that in future sessions Nick would receive one prize per week if he accomplished his goal for that week.

My goals for November 3rd   *mawth words*

11/6

List 4 reasons: why it would
be helpful to talk at school.

1. I cold ansr esyr.
2. I cold talk to my
friends.
3. I could talk things
out.
4. I culd ansr qweshins.

Nick,
These are 4 wonderful reasons
to talk at school and I am
so happy to help you. I know
you will someday and I promise
no one will yell or scream! We
all love you too much!

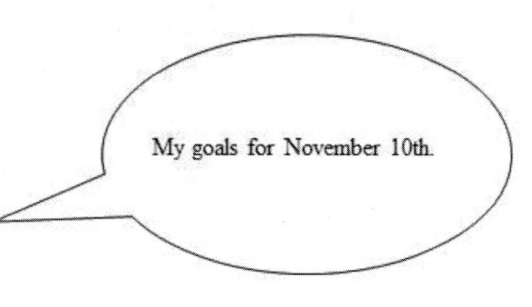

My goals for November 10th.

Class #1

1. Nick brought John to class to play "Language Trivia" again. A choice of activities is provided as choices are important for children with anxiety. Nick mouthed "Yes", "No", and "Green" to answer questions. Nick is competitive and is eager to win the game so that questions requiring answers other than yes and no have been introduced.
2. John and Nick took turns reading every other page of a story while recording it. I had to leave the room as Nick did not want me to hear his voice. We discussed the vocabulary upon completion of the recording.
3. Nick was given an article on Franklinite. He chose a prize and agreed again that in the future he would be awarded one prize a week upon completion of his goal for that week.

Class#2

1. John and Nick finished playing the "Language Trivia" game. Nick mouthed "Yes", "No" and "Blue" three times.
2. Today's journal prompts were: Do you like to play Language Trivia? Why or why not? Nick's response was, "I like it. I like it because you get to go any way you want." Next prompt: How do you feel about mouthing words? Nick's response was, "Ok." Third prompt: I feel proud of myself because____. Nick's response was, "I don't know."
3. A new "Sound Game" was introduced. Sentence strips were prepared ahead of class. Each sentence ended with a sound as, "Be a person who just finished eating and *burp*." Other sentences ended with the words *growl, quack, breathe, gobble, moo, meow, honk, peep, hiss, grunt, bark, squeak, crunch, roar, buzz, zoom, beep, baa, boing, laugh, cry* or *be quiet*. The sentence strips were arranged in order of difficulty for Nick. They were held up one at a time and the boys were to read the sentence strip silently and try to be the first to make the sound. John participated eagerly. Nick only said "*burp*" and "*baa*".

My Goals for November 10th   mawth words

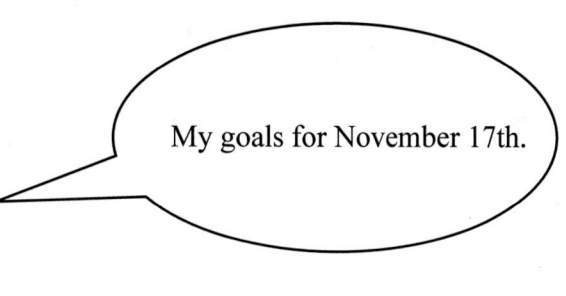

My goals for November 17th.

Class #1

1. Nick, Michael and John came together today. They each wrote a sentence strip of their own for the "Sound Game". Nick tried to avoid a sound and wrote, "Be a T-rex and *stamp*." The boys enjoyed playing the game again. Nick was especially rowdy demonstrating his anxiety about wanting to make the sounds. Each time he discriminates a little more and adds more sounds as he responds to the sentence strips.

Class #2

1. Michael and Nick recorded a story on the computer using the Scholastic, "Wiggle Works" program. Michael and I still have to remain outside the door while Nick is recording even though we know Nick whispers to Michael at lunchtime. These recorded stories will soon be introduced into Nick's regular classroom as a listening center for the other children. Nick's behavior was not good. Directions had to be given several times before he would listen and follow them. The goal sheets will now be sent home each Friday for Nick's parents to be aware of his progress at school.
2. We discussed different animal sounds. Nicholas was instructed to take his journal home and practice making different animal sounds.

Class #3

1. John and Michael played a new board game answering questions with, "Yes, "No" and animal sounds. Questions requiring other verbal answers were, also, presented. Nick mouthed some answers such as, "Thank you." And whispered his answer to John in front of me. Two syllable animal sounds were two syllable "croaks". "Tweet" was not discernible.

My goals for November 17th
Nick would not choose a goal. Therefore, one was chosen for him: Mrs. Kervatt's goal for Nick is to make animal sounds

ok

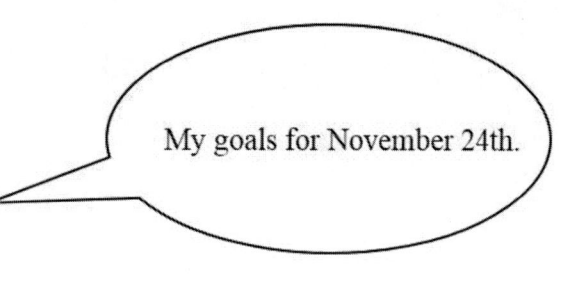

My goals for November 24th.

Class #1

1. Nick came to class by himself today. He wrote a goal for the week. I had to encourage him to try a different goal. He said that he would use his message recorder to answer questions in his regular classroom by the end of the day. We practiced a question answer session, asking each other questions. He accomplished this by writing out questions for me to answer. He mouthed "Yes", "No" and "school". I mouthed some of my answers to point out that it is difficult to read lips!

Class #2

1. Nick was given another journal prompt; How can you make the sounds in our Sound Game different from each other? Nick's response was; "I have no idea...move my mouth different?" We then made a word map of different animal sounds. I wrote the animal name and Nick wrote the sound each animal would make.

2. A list of stories that included animal sounds was obtained by searching the Internet. Some of the books were already in the school library. John and Nick did a shared reading of a story about a cow and a pig. The boys used puppets while I did the reading. John read the pig's dialog while I read the cow's dialog. Nick had chosen to be the cow and say, "Moo", but soon realized that was the more difficult sound for him to produce. He refused to participate and threw the cow puppet. He then chose to participate rather than be sent back to class. His animal sounds were much more distinct today, both in the play and the Sound Game.

Class #3

1. Nick chose a new child, Stephanie, to bring to class. The three of us recorded songs on the karaoke machine. I sang the words and they provided the animal sounds, sometimes jointly and other times individually. The songs were, "On Thanksgiving Day" and "Old MacDonald". Stephanie agreed to take the recording back to the regular classroom so that the whole class could listen and then sing along. Nick was very reluctant to have this done. The recording was, however, played in the classroom. Now the class had heard his voice and Nick could see that no one overreacted.

My goals for November 24th

anmlp sounds Mouthing wrds

Animal Sounds

cat — meow *
bear — grr
turkey — gobbl
fish — blub
bird — twfet *
pig — oinR
duck — Quack
cow — moo

Thanksgiving Day

On Thanksgiving Day, so early in the morn,

I gave a duckling a hand full of corn.

He ate it all. That isn't the end.

He waddled off to find his duckling friends.

Quack, Quack…..Quack, Quack!

Quack, Quack…..Quack, Quack!

He waddled off to find his duckling friends.

On Thanksgiving Day, so early in the morn,

I gave a turkey a hand full of corn.

He ate it all. That isn't the end.

He waddled off to find his barnyard friends.

Gobble, Gobble…..Quack, Quack!

Gobble, Gobble…..Quack, Quack!

He waddled off to find his barnyard friends.

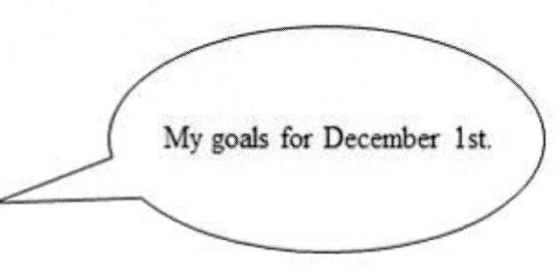

My goals for December 1st.

Class #1

1. Nick wrote his goal for December 1st. Choosing different goals on the goal list is difficult for him. He chose to use puppets to make animal sounds.
2. Nick agreed to call his mom from my room telephone. He seemed pleased with this activity. We wrote suggested ideas in his journal to talk about when he phones.
3. Nick agreed to make more distinct animal sounds this week.
4. Nick mouthed counting numbers to twenty.

Class #2

1. Nick called his mom while I waited outside the closed door. His mom was not at home so he left a message on his own. He used the notes we made in his journal.
2. We reread *The Cow Who Went Oink*. Nick used both puppets and made all the animal sounds while I read the words. Some sounds were discernible and some were not. I suggested that we practice the sounds. Nick went to the other side of the room, behind the bookcase where I could not see him. He made much more distinct sounds from there.

Class #3

1. Nick brought three other children today; John, Stephanie and a new child Christopher. We played the game "Kids on Stage" during which a child pantomimes the object, animal or action on the card that is drawn. I instructed the children to, also, use a sound along with the pantomime. The other children then had to guess what the object, animal or action was. The child guessing the correct answer would become the next actor. This game encouraged Nick to speak in order to state the answer. He mouthed his answers or wrote them on the chalkboard if we could not read his lips. Nick, also, pantomimed a refrigerator, a monkey, blowing bubbles, hammering a nail and a bear.

My goals for December 1st

puppts make annl sounds
Call Mom

Call Mom   337-4945 12/3

1. Hi Mom!

2. I love you

3. I'm calling   From Mrs. Krvck
   room
                 maby my
4. Lunch Soon
dad

Call Toys R US   670-7733 No

1. Do you have the game
   Sale of the Century?

 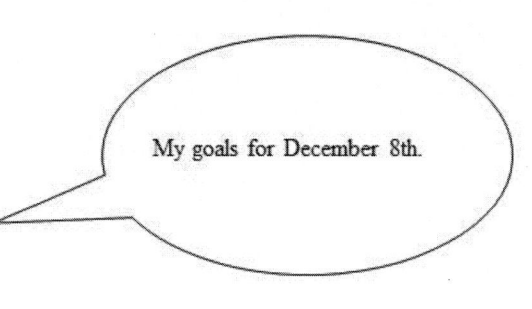

My goals for December 8th.

Class #1

1. We used the karaoke machine to sing a new song, "The Barnyard Song". Nick practiced the sounds that I had written on the chalkboard. He stood behind me and made the sound of the animal name to which I pointed. I would then guess the animal. He did not use his "real voice" to make the sounds and would not attempt to make word sounds such as "bow-wow" or "fiddle-e-fee". He did enjoy making the other animal sounds using the microphone as I sang the words.
2. Nick colored Wiggle Works pictures on the computer. I sat beside him and tried to carry on a conversation during this time; ex. "I see you colored the grass green."
3. Nick was given a homework assignment in his journal. The first question was; List more reasons why it would be helpful to speak at school. His written responses were: "I could answer easier.", "Of course, everything would be easier.", "I could tell other people things.", "I could talk." The second prompt was: Tell how animal sounds are different from speaking? His response was, "They growl. We talk." The third prompt was; List some new animal sounds that you could make. His response: "lion, fish, seal, gorilla".

Class #2

1. We read the big book, *Over in the Meadow*. Nick used puppets to make the animal sounds while I read the text. The sounds he made were a frog (rivet), a bee (buzz), a mouse (squeak) and a duck (quack). The sounds are becoming more distinct. However, the word buzz is difficult for him.
2. Nick called his mom again as he knew she would be home today. I had to stand outside the room. I tried leaving the door open about an inch. However, we spent 15 minutes with me opening the door and Nick closing the door. Nick would hang up the phone and come over to close the door. I could not even leave it open an inch.
3. As per our curriculum, Nick must do a speaking prompt in front of his class. We discussed it. Nick drew a picture of Curious George. He recorded his thoughts about the book character to be played in his classroom the next day.

Class #3

1. We played "Kids on Stage" again. Nick refused to make "zzz" sound of a bee.
2. Nick and I went to his classroom with his picture and recording. He said he wouldn't stand in front of the class. When his name was called, I started the recording and he held his picture up from his desk. The class had been instructed NOT to respond for Nick

---

My goal for December 8th

new anml souns

"Are you coming to my house? Do you have kids?"

 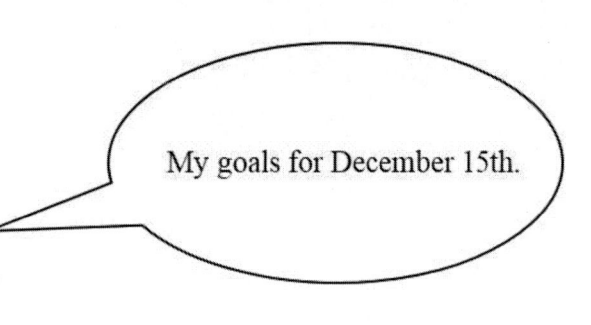

My goals for December 15th.

Class #1

1. Nick wrote a new goal for this week, "Call Mom". I suggested leaving the door open two inches. Nick refused. He called his mom while I waited outside the closed door.
2. The poem, "Careful Connie" by Lois Simmie was introduced to Nick. The message is that Careful Connie is too afraid to do anything. Therefore, she will never have any fun in life. We then rewrote the poem using a poetry frame. The Title was "Risky Nick". The following page demonstrates his writing. Nick took the poem home to share with his family. His mother sent back a note stating that it helped to initiate a good conversation about taking risks and trying new things. We both hope it will have an impact on Nick's speaking in school.

Class #2

1. Nick wrote a message on the chalkboard requesting to call his mother. I complied, but he refused again to leave the door open even one inch.
2. Nick finished coloring the Wiggle Works story he had been creating on the computer. I sat by his side and he made a grunt sound whenever he made a mistake.
3. We read *Over in the Meadow.* Nick used puppets again to make all the animal sounds using the table as a stage. Nick sat under the table and held up each puppet as it was called for. All sounds were much better, including "zzz".

Class #3

1. Nick and John came to class. We played a game called, "Animal Lotto". The boys were instructed to make the animal sound or say the name of the animal before picking up the matching card. Nick made many animal sounds and said some words in a throaty or gruff voice. He said, "Toucan, one, two, three and thank you". He and John talked baby talk or nonsense words back and forth, for example, ba, ba, and da. Nick seems to be trying out some verbalization in my presence. He may be getting bored with animal sounds. My response is always no response, so as not to put any attention on him. Nick was much more verbal today than usual, but made sure he had closed the door before we played the game so that no one else could hear him. He, also, mouthed words today.

My goals for December 15th

call mom

CAREFUL CONNIE

Careful Connie's terrified
Of accidents and ills,
Of gyms and germs and things that squirm,
Heights and depths and heat and chills;
Of bicycles and buses,
Cats and cows and lakes and hills,
Flying things and furry things;

So Careful Connie never will . . .

Climb a tree might fall down
Go swimming might drown
Play in the rain might get muddy
Play games might get bloody
Cross the street might get hit
Pet a dog might get bit
Eat candy might get a toothache
Eat pizza might get a bellyache
Read a book might ruin her eyes
Say hello might have to say goodbye

Careful Connie's oh, so carefully
Sitting in her room,
She's absolutely safe there,
Just sitting in the gloom.
She never laughs and never cries,
She never falls and bumps her head,
She's going to live forever
But she might as well be . . . .

LOIS SIMMIE

RISKY

Risky _____Nick_____ **isn't afraid**
Of
dogs, rats, Dark,
school techersers,
candy, gar,
pools, me, books,
and pants, books,

So Risky _____Nick_____ **will**
play with dogs
and cats, ignor
the Dark, I will
play at school
I will swimr
in pools, I will
ware pants

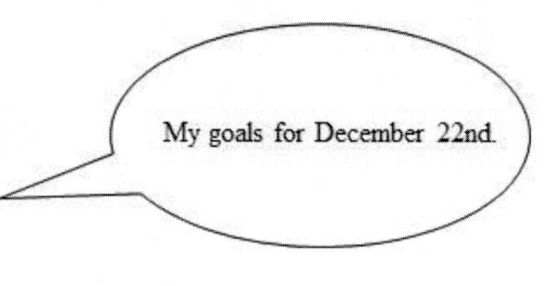

My goals for December 22nd.

Class #1

1. Nick performed his puppet show, *Over in the Meadow,* for his past kindergarten teacher. He sat under the table and held the puppets up as he made the animal sounds. He appeared very pleased to have her there.
2. Nick insisted on playing "Word Munchers" on the computer.
3. We played a "Holiday Trivia" game with Christopher. Nick mouthed the answers. He wouldn't use his throat voice.

Class #2

Nick's class had their holiday party so class was canceled.

Class #3

Holiday Recess

My goals for December 22nd

MOuthing
wourds

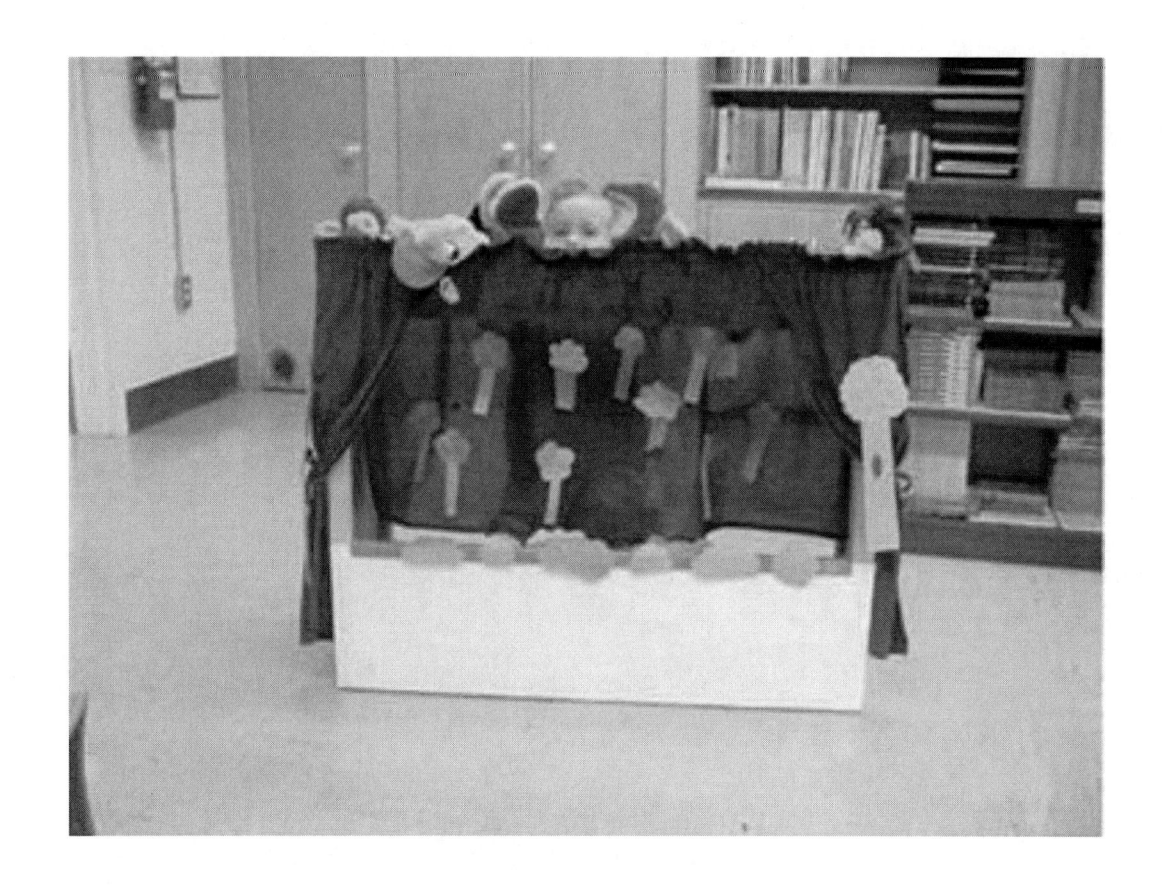

The frog croaked, "Rivet, rivet." The duck quacked, "Quack, Quack."

Nicholas
Goals for Communication
January

Make animal sounds with songs, books or puppets.
Dates 1/19, 1/22, 1/26, 1/27, 2/2

Play "Word Munchers" on the computer and make vowel sounds.
Dates 1/14, 1/15, 1/22, 1/26, 1/27, 2/2, 2/9

Record and play a speaking prompt for the regular classroom.
Dates 1/12

Class with Mrs. Kervatt three times a week to record on the computer using "Wiggle Works" computer program. Listen with a partner and Mrs. Kervatt.
Dates 2/10, 2/23

Play board games using two voice messengers to answer Yes and No questions.
Dates 10/28, 11/3

Mouth "Yes" and "No" to answer board game questions.
Dates 11/4, 11/5, 11/10, 11/11, 11/17 (red), 11/20 (animal sounds), 11/24, 1/5

Use puppets to make animal sounds.
Dates 11/26, 12/3, 12/10, 12/17, 12/23

Whisper "Yes" and "No" to answer board game questions.
Dates _____

Record with Mrs. Kervatt outside the slightly open door.
Dates _____

Record with Mrs. Kervatt or a friend in the room.
Dates _____

Use message recorders to answer Yes and No questions in the classroom.
Dates _____

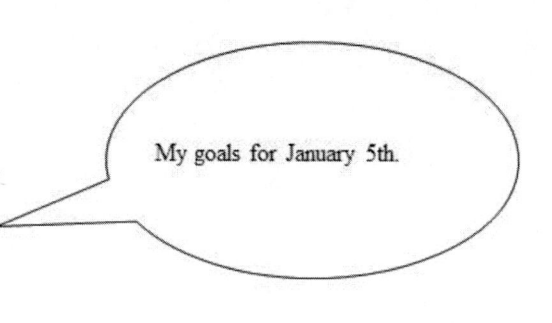

My goals for January 5th.

Class #1

1. Nick seems to have regressed somewhat over the holiday break. He would not choose a goal of those suggested on the new goal sheet. He said he would think of one by the next class.
2. Nick mouthed all communication, but was frustrated when I could not understand. He then wrote what he wanted to say on the chalkboard. We played "Language Trivial Pursuit" to which Nick mouthed the answers. He insisted on taking a prize today instead of waiting until Thursday, but did say, "Bye, Bye" in his throat voice as he left the classroom.

Class #2

1. Nick's goal is to mouth words again. He agreed to change the goal next week. We played "Language Trivia" for fifteen minutes. Nick mouthed the answers.
2. After a fire drill he wanted to play "Word Munchers" on the computer. He was instructed to say the vowel sound presented at the top of the game board as each new game started. He did so for the two sounds of "oo" in his throat voice. He, also, said, "Darn" in his throat voice when he made a mistake. Nick agreed to play a new game in the future with a group of seven children from another second grade class who usually arrive early and watch Nick play "Word Munchers."
3. A journal prompt was given for homework. The prompt was: Tell about some situations or problems caused by not speaking that have happened at school. His response was, "People are bugging me".

Class #3

1. Nick and I together added and changed some of the goals on his October goal sheet. We added whisper and make vowel sounds. Nick played "Word Munchers" on the computer. He said the long and short vowel sounds for "a" quite clearly.
2. The seven students who are scheduled with me after Nick's class arrived. We played the "Sound Game" for ten minutes with them. Nick easily made animal sounds with the other students. It has taken three months to get to this point, but Nick has now expanded his realm of people who are allowed to hear him speak, or in this case, make a sound.

My goals for January 5th   *nothing words*

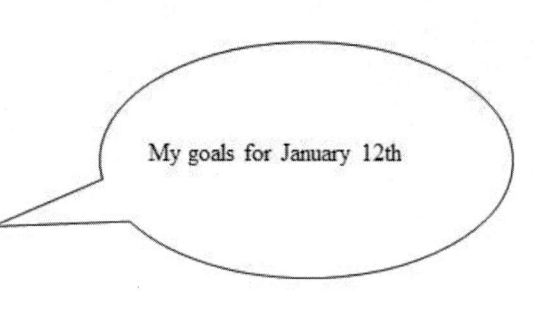

My goals for January 12th

Class #1

1. We started to make a book using Nick's journal suggestions for "Why I Should Speak". Nick made sounds during the process, but few were discernible.
2. Nick wrote a note to me to say that he got a guinea pig for the holidays and made a squeak sound indicating the sound it makes.
3. Nick wanted to play a simulation computer game and in order to do so, he agreed to whisper this week

Class #2

1. We continued working on the book, "Why I Should Speak". Nick wrote his goal "wisper". He stood in the corner with his back to me and whispered, "Play Word Munchers." I had to keep the room's distance between us and ask him to say it louder. He did so louder the second time. He was then allowed to play the game for the remainder of the period.

Class #3

1. Nick came to class with a group of seven children from another classroom to play "Kids on Stage". Nick was very quiet at first, but very willing to pantomime and make sounds. He, also, made some sounds while observing, appearing to be testing the responses of the other children. All children associated with Nick have been instructed not to overreact when he verbalizes and they complied.
2. Nick took my toy voice enhancer megaphone home for a prize to use for two days. He knelt in the corner under the desk and whispered, "Yes, please" very softly when I asked if he would like to take the enhancer home for the weekend.

My goals for January 12th

wisper

 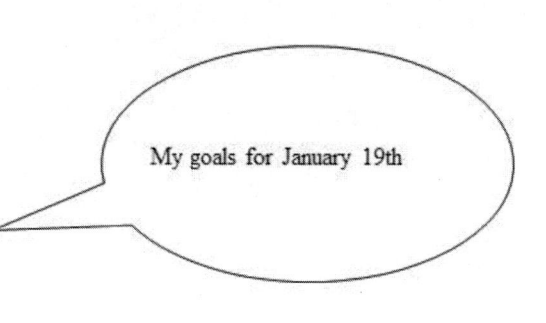

My goals for January 19th

Class #1

1. The book, *Wake Up Sleeping Beauty* was read jointly. Nick made the sounds whistle, cymbals, guitar, gong, drill and kiss as the rest of the text was read to him from the popup book. His sounds were then compared to the book sound chip sounds. He was encouraged to copy the sounds he heard. These are more difficult than animal sounds since most are actual words using onomonopia.
2. Nick spied the new puppet theatre and wanted to use it, probably to avoid practicing the new book sounds. The text from, *I know an Old Lady* was read to him while he used the puppets to make the animal sounds. He did, however, say "Bye, Bye," as he left the room.

Class #2

1. A journal prompt was completed. The first prompt asked: Who else would you like to speak to or whisper besides John, Michael or Chris? Nick's response was, "You". The second prompt asked: Why? Nick's response was, "Cause you make talking fun!!".
2. Nick wrote and illustrated a new book about problems caused at school by not speaking. He titled it, *Don't Try to Make Me Talk*. The text read, "Some of my cousins tried to make me talk. They put me in my bed and tickled me." He grunted, "Uh hum" and "uh huh" for yes and no. Nick asked for an extra copy so that he could have one for his younger brother.

Class #3

1. John came to class with Nick to play, "Animal Lotto". Nick has been whispering to his therapist at their weekly sessions outside of the school setting. He has, also, been seen secretly whispering to John at lunch. He was requested to whisper the name of the animal today. He refused. He was then requested to make an animal sound when a match was not made and to whisper the name of the animals to John when a match was made. He whispered quite loudly and didn't appear to mind that he could be heard by me. Nick made many noises and said some discernible words while playing. He whispered, "Hello," three times in order to take his prize.

My goals for January 19th

Same as last week
whisper

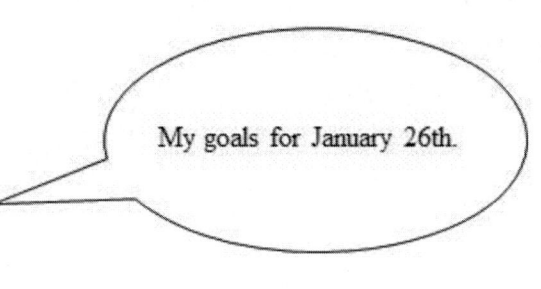

My goals for January 26th.

Class #1

1. Nick wrote his new goal for this week as "whispering". We used the new puppet theatre to pantomime the book, *Tittle Tattle Goose*. Nick said, "Tittle Tattle," for the goose using his throat voice. He also said, "moo, quack, cock-a-doodle, and neigh," much more clearly.
2. Nick was anxious to play a computer game and whispered to me, "Play Bouncing Balls." I sat much closer to him at the computer.

Class #2

1. Nick's mother had requested a visit by me to the family home so as to continue to build a rapport with Nick and his younger brother. Nick discussed the visit with me, mouthing that he would show me his computer games.
2. We used the puppet theatre again acting out *Tittle Tattle Goose*. Nick used his throat voice to make the sounds.
3. A new story was introduced, *Scratch the Dog*, in which Nick made the sound effects in his throat voice. He said, "Scratch, ding, rattle, hip-hop," which were highlighted in the story.
4. Nick played "Thinking Things" on the computer and while facing sideways, he whispered, "Play Thinking Things."

Class #3

Nick was absent today.

My goals for January 26th   wispring

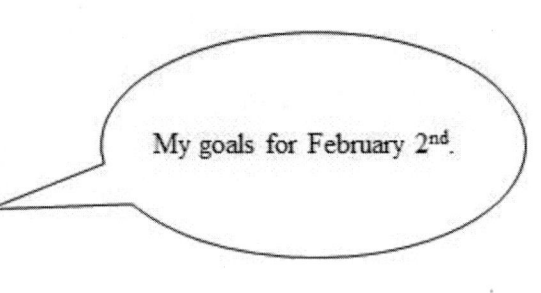

My goals for February 2nd.

Class #1

1. The following sounds were introduced, reviewed and practiced: moo, buzz, pop, eek, who, clop, dribble, cock-a-doodle-doo, boom, splat, tick-tock, sizzle, blurp, knock, and slurp. Nick supplied the sounds for the book, *Mr. Brown Can Moo, Can You?*.
2. Nick stood in the corner and I sat closer, in my desk chair with my back to him. Questions such as, "Where do you live? How old are you? What is your phone number?" were asked of him. Nick whispered the answers and was then instructed to ask his own questions. He whispered, "Are you coming to my house?" This is a big step in progression by his initiating speech. He then played a computer game as a reward.

Class #2

1. *Mr. Brown Can Moo, Can You?* was reread using the theatre and puppets. Upon encountering the words, "He can whisper like a butterfly, can you?" Nick wouldn't whisper. He did, however, stick his head out of the theatre window and say, "Hello," four times in his throat voice. He may be testing my response now to his voice and as always the response is to continue on with no overreaction.
2. Using the karaoke machine again, we sang and recorded the song, "The Wheels on the Bus." The sound words had been written on the board so that Nick would know the order of the sounds. Nick made the sounds when the microphone was held in front of him. The final verses contained the words "move on back, up and down and open shut." Nick sang these words reluctantly in a muffled voice.
3. Nick whispered answers to my questions from the corner with our backs to each other. He then played a computer game for his reward.

Class #3

1. John and Stephanie joined us for class. The game, "Figuratively Speaking" was played with true/false questions. Nick would answer in his throat voice or go to the other side of the room and whisper softly while facing the group of two children. Later, he moved closer and behind the puppet theatre, visible from the waist up. He requested to mouth the words instead, but was reminded that this week's goal was to whisper. Nick was very verbal today using his throat voice and continued talking to John and Stephanie as the door was opened and they walked back to their classroom.

My goals for February 2nd   sound   whisper

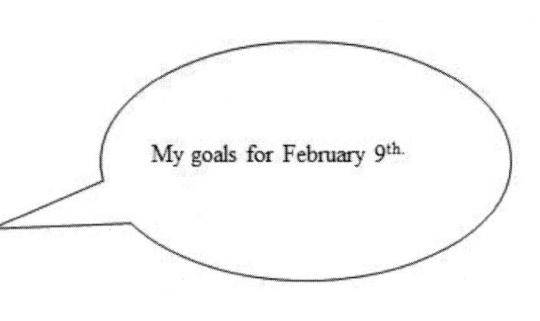

My goals for February 9th.

Class #1

1. The goal "whispering" was again chosen by Nick for this week.
2. The regular classroom teacher requested that we practice. "The Weed Song" which Nick was to perform along with a small group of children in the second grade play on March 27th. The song was practiced twice using the karaoke machine. Nick barely mouthed the words, even though they had been practiced in music class many times and he knew them. He would not do the hand movements stating that he doesn't like to dance.
3. We played "Kid Phonics" scrambled word game. I had to encourage Nick to whisper answers.
4. Nick again stood in the corner to whisper to me, but this time he used the toy megaphone to answer two of the three questions.

Class #2

1. Nick recorded seven pages from *Look Alike Animals* on the computer program, "Wiggle Works". He chose to be in the room by himself. His recording reflected enthusiasm.
2. The amount of prizes from the list that had been developed with Nick's mother were beginning to be low. Nick was given the opportunity to choose inexpensive items from a catalog to be ordered as new rewards. Nick's job was to state the page number, catalog number, price and description of the item he wanted so that I could write them on the order form. He was very verbal using his throat voice as we completed the order form.
3. Nick played "Punctuation Game" on the computer, talking in his throat voice as he placed punctuation marks.
4. Nick helped to carry new books downstairs for his reading group to use. He was given an extra copy with the choice of taping the stories at home or using his voice in the classroom by reading aloud with his group. He does not like extra homework. Therefore, this should be a good incentive to begin using his voice in the classroom.

Class #3

1. Nick, John and Stephanie played the game "Figuratively Speaking" again. Nick spoke the entire time in his throat voice, including saying, "Goodbye," as he left the room. No prompting was needed. However, he did close the door at one point stating that he was being too loud.

My goals for February 9th   4his pring

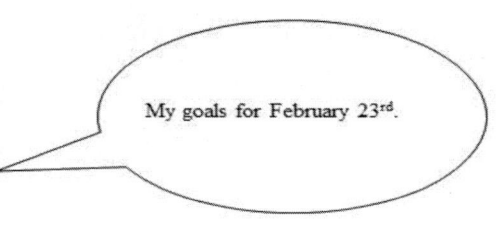

My goals for February 23rd.

Class #1

1. Nick came to class speaking in his throat voice. He chose from three activities mentioned to finish recording *Look-Alike Animals* from Scholastic "Wiggle Works" and then used the tools to paint the pictures. He knows that this recording is to be transferred to his classroom computer to be used as a listening center by the other children. He is rather reluctant to do this. While coloring, he did much talking in his throat voice. This is one of the first times he has voluntarily initiated speech rather than repeating words that have been requested.
2. Journal assignment: Find comic strip frames that show SOUND words. Cut them out. Glue them here. Highlight the sound words. Practice the words to say at school.

Class #2

1. Nick did a nice job with his journal assignment. He used his throat voice to say, "Woof, zzzzzzz and pat".
2. An individual reading inventory was explained to Nick and he was requested to read for me. He read the first part silently and answered all questions in his throat voice. He was requested to read the second part aloud. He read a few sentences in his throat voice and the rest silently. He answered the next eight questions in his throat voice, jokingly asking if he got one hundred percent. He stated that maybe he would read the word recognition word list another day.
3. We sorted the prize box toys. Nick did much talking in his gruff throat voice. I consulted The Selective Mutism Group forum with my concern about the gruff voice. The doctor emailed back stating that this looked like a step forward, or a phase, until Nick would move into his real voice.
4. Nick had written four questions in his journal to be used during our question/answer time. He went to the corner and used his throat voice to ask the questions and then requested to do them again using the toy megaphone.
5. The next group arrived to my classroom and we all practiced the class play song with words and hand movements. Nick seemed more willing to do this today.

Class #3

1. Nick played a vocabulary board game with a different second grade group of seven children. He agreed that in order to play, he would read the word and use it in a sentence. He did so in his throat voice which seemed a little less gruff. He did not hesitate to speak to the other children in this voice.

My goals for February 23rd   *Yes or no   wisp r*

Find some comic strip frames that show SOUND words. Cut them out. Glue them here. Highlight the sound words. Practice them to show me.

Great job!

44

Nicholas
Goals for Communication
March

Say Yes or No or a word with a sentence to answer board game questions.

Dates 2/27, 3/6, 4/17, 4/20, 5/1, 5/8

Stand in the corner and whisper to Mrs. Kervatt to answer questions.

Dates 1/13, 1/15, 1/22, 1/26, 1/27, 2/5, 2/6

Use your voice to play a game.

Dates 2/12

Class with Mrs. Kervatt three times a week to record on the computer using Scholastic Wiggle Works computer program. Listen with a partner and Mrs. Kervatt.

Dates 2/10, 2/23

Read reading placement word list aloud.

Dates 3/2 (4.0 GL), 3/31 (6.0 GL)

Stand in the corner facing forward and ask Mrs. Kervatt questions to her back.

Dates 3/1

Say people words (dialog) with puppets using songs or a story using different voices.

Dates 3/3 (alien), 4/21 (old woman), 4/28 (old man), 5/5 (Darth Vader)

Record in the classroom with Mrs. Kervatt outside, leaving the door open 2 inches.

Dates 4/17, 4/21, 4/27, 5/8

Read part of a story and say one word in real voice.

Dates

Record a story with Mrs. Kervatt or a friend in the room.

Dates

Use message recorders to answer Yes or No questions in the classroom.

Dates

Call Mom and leave the door open 2 inches.

Dates

Speak to the Grade Three teacher at our game time.

Dates 4/17, 4/24

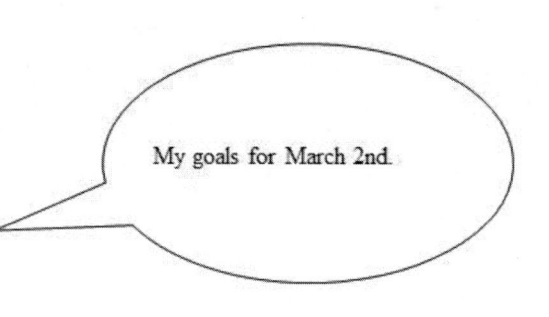

My goals for March 2nd.

Class #1

1. Together, we wrote new goals for the spring, including: Say one word in your real voice. Nick only agreed to two of the goals: Stand in the corner and ask Mrs. Kervatt questions and Read the word recognition lists.
2. Nick read two Grade 4 word lists in his throat voice. He knows that this activity is to determine his word recognition level for reading placement.
3. Nick whispered three questions from the corner. My back was to him. He had to be prompted to ask questions with the suggested topic of, "My Pet".
4. He experimented with the "Kid Pix" computer program talking in his throat voice to demonstrate its use to me.
5. Nick said, "Bye" in his throat voice as he left the classroom.

Class #2

1. *Zounds! The Kids' Guide to Sound Making* by Frederick R. Newman was introduced. The book contains examples of sounds by topics such as, "farm sounds" along with directions and illustrations for making the sounds. Also, it has short plays for each topic with the sound words highlighted. Nick chose to read, "Behind the Moon" and play the part of the alien. His throat voice worked well with the alien dialog.
2. We practiced the farm animal sounds from Zounds! By reading the directions and trying to follow them. The sounds were modeled for Nick and then he was instructed to imitate, such as, "bok, bok, bok" for a chicken. He did so, but with little inflection, except for high and low. We, then, read *The Little Red Hen*. Nick played the duck, dog, cat and pig using his own funny dialog to answer with little difference in pitch.
3. A Grade One student arrived for my next class and Nick performed the last page for her.

Class #3

1. Nick arrived with six children: Michael and Maia from his class and four children from a different second grade classroom. He is being prepared to interact with other children who may be in his third grade class next year. We played a vocabulary board game. Nick was very verbal during the entire class, being very silly at times. He did not hesitate to talk in an almost normal voice. The group responded well, but Nick needed to be reminded to be respectful to a teacher.

My goals for March 2nd   wisper qustons

 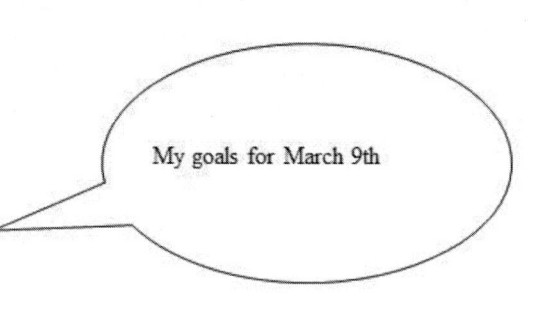

My goals for March 9th

Class #1

1. Nick agreed to record another story on "Wiggle Works" for his classroom. He chose *Wake up Scooterville.* I explained to him that we did not have to rewrite the text, but he wanted to do so and typed in family names for the characters. Then, he told me to, "Move on out!" so that he could record without me in the room. He stopped recording when I had to come in at one point to get some staples and then he redid the page when I left. He recorded five pages of the story in his real voice.
2. Nick offered to help me punch out letters for a bulletin board. I said, "Isn't it wonderful that you can tell me what you want?" He replied, "No. I'd rather be on the computer!"

Class #2

1. We continued rewriting and recording *Wake up Scooterville.* Nick spoke in a softer throat voice throughout. When asked how his throat felt, re replied, "Better." I casually said, "If you would talk higher up in your throat, it won't get so sore."
2. Nick has not completed his homework from last week. The journal assignment was: Think of some different voices you could use besides animal or insect voices. Write some questions to ask Mrs. Kervatt. Nick went back to his classroom to get it. He had listed more animals so we rewrote the list. He wrote: Darth Vader, an old man and an old lady.

Class #3

1. Nick arrived speaking in his throat voice with a prearranged group of children. He helped to carry the game, "Figuratively Speaking," to the table and informed everyone that he would be first because he chose the game. Then, he sat in the teacher chair and had to be encouraged to move to a student chair. He was very talkative during the session and stated that he was being silly. He only used his throat voice today.

My goals for March 9th   wisper austols

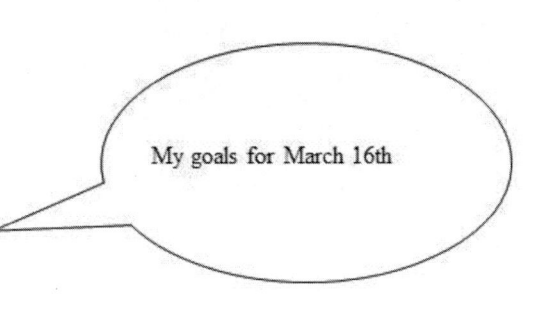

My goals for March 16th

Class #1

1. A new goal for this week was chosen: Use different voices. We talked about the last homework assignment and Nick was instructed to write dialog for Darth Vader, the old man and the old woman. He was given materials to take home to make puppets for the characters.

Class #2

1. Nick arrived prepared with his puppets and dialog. We talked while he added yarn hair to the puppets. Nick insisted that the tongue be removed from the old woman puppet that I had made. We spoke a little about his grandparents and how their voices sound different from each other so that this could be applied to his speaking using the old man puppet and the old woman puppet.

2. Nick opened the word processor on the computer and typed eight lines of random letters. Then, he let me type the dialog from his journal to write a play. He had a hard time adding a title and setting. Nick got restless, or possibly anxious, proceeding with our activity with the puppets and so we stopped.

3. We began our question/answer session. Nick asked the questions he had written in his journal from the corner, facing forward and using the toy megaphone. He asked, "Do you have a kid?", "What is his name?" and "What is your favorite color?" He seemed less anxious asking questions than he has in the past.

Class #3

1. Nick walked upstairs with the group of seven children from different second grade classes. We played a board game, "Songs We Sing". The students had to move along the game board using dice to determine the number of jumps and then landing upon a song description such as, "It's about an old man who owns a farm." Next, the child had to name the song and sing the first line. Nick was hesitant to sing. It was difficult for him to sing using his throat voice. Instead, he said some of the words while I sang the tune. He stated that he hated the game, but he was cooperative.

My goals for March 16th

use different voices

 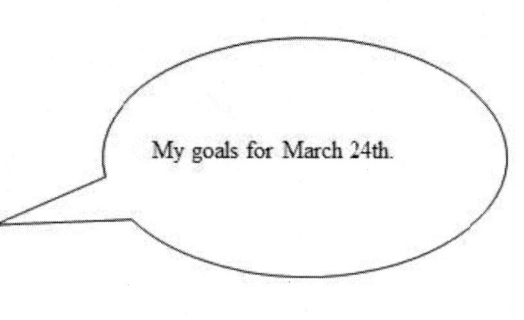

My goals for March 24th.

Class #1

Professional Day

Class #2

1. The goal Nick chose and wrote for this week is, "dialog".
2. Nick chose a board game ahead of time to play on Thursday. It's obvious that he thinks ahead of time to manipulate and control a speaking situation. He "hated" last week's game involving songs and so made sure he chose the game for this week. This may be related to his uneasiness about singing "The Weed Song" in the school play.
3. Nick dictated the rest of his play as I typed it for him. He had to be encouraged to contribute dialog and asked if he was going to have to perform this play in his classroom. I assured him that he would not have to do that. We acted out the short play. Nick took the old man and the old woman characters. He used a different pitch voice more easily, but still used his throat voice for the old woman.
4. As a reward, Nick played "Word Munchers" on the computer. He used his throat voice to say each word that his word muncher ate.

Class #3

1. A mixed group arrived with Nick to play "Sale of the Century" board game. Nick overheard one child state that he had had no breakfast. Nick offered to share his colored cereal with everyone. He asked each child what color they wanted and gave them their choice. Nick was very verbal during the game using his throat voice. He seems to be listening and responding in a more relaxed way without focusing so much on the act of speaking.

My goals for March 24th   dilog

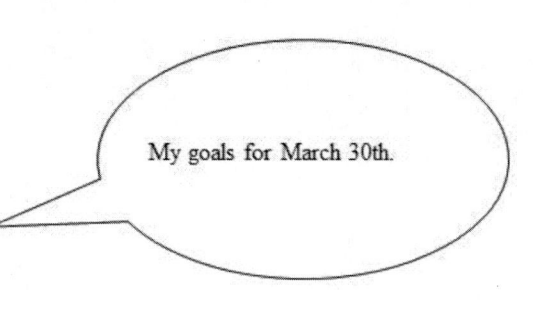

My goals for March 30th.

Class #1

1. Nicholas rerecorded half of *"Wake up Scooterville"* on the "Wiggle Works" computer program. He would not allow me to stay in the room.
2. We discussed his class play and practiced the song, "We're Weeds, We're Cool!"
3. We discussed cutting down to two sessions. Nicholas stated that this would be a good idea so that he could have more time to finish his classroom seatwork.
4. Nick chose to read some more of the word recognition lists for reading placement. He then wrote this as his goal for the week.

Class #2

1. The "Wiggle Works" recording was completed.
2. During our question/answer session Nick tried to ask questions, but could think of few. He stood directly behind me while responding in his throat voice with short answers to most of my questions.
3. Nick read four more word recognition word lists in his throat voice, completing sixth grade words with a seventy-five percent accuracy. He is very proud of his reading ability.

Class #3

Assembly

My goals for March 30th

Word List

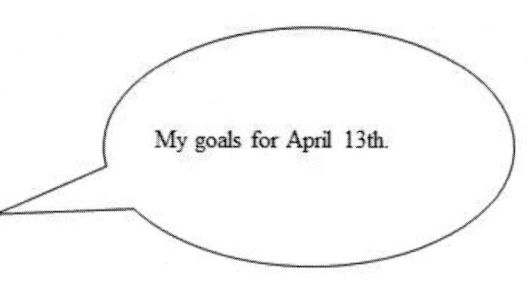

My goals for April 13th.

Class #1

District Meeting

Class #2

1. Nick wrote a new goal for this week: Tape record with the door open!
2. We wrote Scene Two of the "Darth Story" and added Nick as a character. He elaborated slightly more with details. Details are still very difficult for him. We discussed story structure such as character, setting, problem and solution. Nick suggested taking the play home to finish with the help of his younger brother.
3. We went next door to the next classroom to ask the teacher for a computer disk. No other students were in the classroom. However, Nick would not ask for the disk. He played the game when we returned to our classroom. Nick's voice was more relaxed today.

Class #3

1. Nick came to class early to complete his goal: Tape record with the door open. He changed his mind, however, and wanted to wait until after class.
2. The group arrived and a volunteer was requested to go get the third grade teacher to join our game. The motive was to have Nick speak to her so that he could begin the next year with no anxiety over his new teacher hearing him speak. We played a vocabulary game. The students were to say the word and use it in a sentence for the first round. Nick did not hesitate to speak in his throat voice with the new teacher present. During the second round, the students were to use the vocabulary word they landed on to ask the third grade teacher a question about third grade. Nick did this with no problem. However, he may have been a little anxious as he hit his head with the sponge dice at one point and began to act silly.
3. After the group left, Nick agreed to record with the door open slightly. He asked me, however, to go next door into the book room and close the door so that he could not be heard. He recorded, "Hi" in his normal voice!

My goals for April 13th

Tape record with door open

My goals for April 20th.

Class #1

District Meeting

Nick was reminded to bring his puppets and complete Scene Two of his play for use on Wednesday.

Class #2

1. Nick stated that he had forgotten the puppets. Therefore, my puppets were used. Nick closed the door. He portrayed Darth, the old man and Nick. He differentiated the voices at first, but went back to the same voice for all characters shortly afterward.
2. Nick recorded three words in his real voice with the door open slightly. He still requested me to leave the room and we modified the amount of inches the door would be open for some time.
3. A computer game was played as a reward.

Class #3

1. Another third grade teacher joined the group to play a decoding skill game. Each child volunteered "gh" words that were then written on the board. Next, the children took turns coming to the board to cross out the gh in each word and we sang a song with "ght" words. The group played a board game with "gh" words and each child asked the third grade teacher a question about third grade using the word they landed on. Nick readily asked his questions while looking at the teacher. He had to be spoken to after class, however, about his behavior such as pretending to sleep on the table.
2. Nick was notified that our sessions would now be cut down to two times a week.

My goals for April 20th   *Door open*

My goals for April 27th.

Class #1

1. Nick wrote his goal as "same thing" for this week.
2. He recorded four words on the recorder with the door open a little. I stood outside of the door rather than going into the room next door.
3. Nick performed the "Darth Vader" play. He portrayed Darth and Nick. There was some discrimination between the two voices. Nick stated that he will continue writing and add Scene Three to include his younger brother as a character.
4. Nick played a computer game as a reward. He was very cooperative today.

Class #2

1. "Phonics Rummy" was played with a group. Nicholas was very verbal using a softer throat voice. Surprisingly, he slipped into his real voice in the cafeteria today when he spoke to me. He may not have realized it.
2. Journal assignment prompt: List five things you think or hope third grade will bring. Example: friends you'd like to have in your class; the kind of a teacher you would like; the kinds of books you would like to read.

My goals for April 27th

Same thing.

My goals for May 4th.

Class #1

1. Nick did not want to choose a new goal, even though he was notified that he will only continue with our sessions until May 25th at which time my classes are discontinued so that I can begin reading placement testing with all the children in the school.
2. We acted out Scene Three of Nick's "Darth" play. He performed quite well and spoke as "Nick" for the first time almost in his real voice.
3. We discussed Nick's journal entry to the prompt: List five things you hope third grade will bring. His responses were: 1. I would like to have Mike in my class. 2. I want Magic Tree books. 3. I'd like a nice teacher. 4. I'd like a perfect teacher. 5. I'd like to learn about animals. It might be a good idea to have each child who will be in Nick's third grade class record their own expectations, including Nick, to be played the first day of class in September.
4. Nick played a computer game as a reward.

Class #2

1. A small group of children played a phonics board game. I had to enforce game rules today as all the children were being too physical and loud. Nick is now very comfortable with the mixed group, including some children from another second grade. He speaks in his throat voice without any hesitation.
2. Nick stayed after the group left and was asked to record his journal entry about third grade. He had to be encouraged to do this and spoke very quietly doing the recording.
3. A new journal prompt was assigned.

My goals for May 4th

Same thing

My goals for May 11th.

Class #1

1. Nick wrote his goal for this week as "same thing" again. He did not return his new journal prompt: How has it been helpful to speak at school? How has school changed?
2. Nick was informed that he would be recording his expectations for third grade again because the first recording was not loud enough. He asked why he couldn't just say them next year. I let him know that would be wonderful, but for now his psychologist had suggested this and the new teacher would be doing a project with the recording. With some resistance he recorded again with the door open one inch.
3. Nick played a computer game as a reward. While doing this, a third grade student arrived to deliver something. He watched Nick play the game and talked with him briefly.

Class #2

1. Our small group played a vocabulary game. Nick had to be reminded to remain in his chair like the other children. He willingly cooperated. He was actually speaking in his real voice most of the time. I did not comment on it which would have focused attention on him. Our last meeting is next week.
2. Instructions with prompts for summer writing and speaking in the community were sent home with Nick. His parents are expecting this and will work with him during the summer.

My goals for May 11th

Same thing

My goals for May 18th.

Class #1

1. The last journal prompt was discussed: How has it been helpful to speak at school? How has school changed: Nick wrote: "I could talk to friends, I could answer questions, I could ask questions." The ability to communicate and answer questions is obviously very important to Nick and most likely a great incentive since he has written this response many times throughout the year. Another reason may be because he is quite a bright child, as many SM children are, and therefore, he would be highly motivated to contribute to classroom discussions.
2. Nick wrote his goal for today: What I did last week.
3. Nick agreed to record using his real voice. We negotiated the number of inches to leave the door open. Books had to be placed against the door to keep it from opening more than one inch! Nick's voice on the recording was slightly soft, but audible.
4. Nick played a game on the computer as a reward.
5. We discussed Nick's family visiting my home this summer and taking a trip to an iron mine to see the florescent minerals that I had shown him in the fall. This time he will see them in a real mine. Nick seemed excited and eager to do this.

My goals for May 18th

What I did last week.

5/5 How has it been helpful to talk at school? How has school changed? I could talk to friends. I could awnser questins. I could ask questons

Chapter Five
Epilogue

As Nicholas became more comfortable with speaking in a small group setting, he incorporated some speech into his regular classroom during the end of his second grade year. The monetary goal sheet provided by his private psychologist did not seem to be effective in the fall and was eventually discontinued. Nick had requested that the classroom teacher keep it hidden in her desk as it was an embarrassment to him. Possibly, it may have been more useful toward the end of the school year. His classroom teacher tried many different strategies to coax Nicholas to speak. Even though he was speaking frequently in his throat voice in my individual and small group setting and he was always eager to raise his hand to answer a question in his classroom of twenty-three children, the silence within always quickly took over in that setting.

Toward spring of the school year, Nicholas started whispering answers to his friend in the classroom to be imparted to the rest of the class during discussions. He was requested by his classroom teacher to not only write his regular homework, but also to record reading selections and answers to questions that had been discussed in class that day. Nick did not like the extra work and came to realize that his nonverbal behavior was affecting the amount of homework he received each day.

In addition, Nick was requested to participate in phonics skills review in his throat voice during reading group time. The teacher would call on Nick, just as she did the other children, to make phonetic sounds, then syllable sounds and finally put the syllables together to make a word. Poetry was used to practice the sounds and after requesting Nick to read the name of a poem, "Puddle", several times, he, one day, became so angry that he blurted out, "Puddle!". Speaking in his classroom appeared to come more easily after this incident, but the fear was still noticeably present.

Something happened to Nicholas that spring of his second grade year. Perhaps, the key was to start using some strategies with one child in another classroom, expand the number of people to whom Nick would speak in a small group situation, develop diverse activities and materials, give Nick choices and reward goals that were accomplished. These strategies, in

collaboration with the private psychologist, the parents and the classroom teacher gave Nick a new life.

The process and eventual outcome took seven months, one small step at a time. Everyone involved, including Nick at times, experienced frustration, but realized that patience was the most important factor in helping Nick to overcome his fear. There was a fine line between pressure and encouragement to take the next step. That line had to be discovered by all involved.

Nick, fearlessly, walked into my home with his family in July of that year and began playing with the dog. He was speaking in his normal voice and continues to do so to this day. All school and psychologist's intervention was discontinued at the end of second grade. His parents have continued to introduce him to outside social settings such as recreation camp, sports and making inquiries while on vacation. Doing so will help him to become comfortable with those situations with which he will have to deal throughout his life.

Nicholas had a very successful third grade experience, never failing to contribute to all verbal activities within the classroom and school. He now asks and answers questions without hesitation. The classroom teacher stated that had she not been notified of his anxiety disorder prior to his entering her class, she never would have been aware of any difficulties. She often had to remind herself that this was a child who had a serious anxiety disorder that affected his ability to produce speech, historically, very resistant to intervention.

Upon considering all the frustrations, difficulties and insecurities on my part in the beginning, working with Nicholas proved to be one of the most challenging and rewarding experiences of my career. His story demonstrates the complexity of the selective mute's anxiety disorder. Optimistically, however, it also points out that a school intervention and accommodations in one case, without the use of medication, can work and will persist. The door is now open for Nicholas and his story is one of success.

Resources

Books and Poetry

Bernard, Robin, *Look Alike Animals,* Scholastic Inc., 1994.

Galdone, Paul, *The Little Red Hen,* Houghton Mifflin, 1985.

I Know an Old Lady, Little Golden Books Family Entertainment, 1995.

Keats, Ezra Jack, *Over in the Meadow,* Viking Penguin, 1999.

Most, Bernard, *The Cow That Went Oink,* Harcourt Brace, 1990.

Newman, Frederick, R., *Zounds! The Kid's Guide to Sound Making,* Random House, 1983.

Seuss, Dr., *Mr. Brown Can Moo, Can You? Dr. Seuss's Book of Wonderful Noises,* Bright and Early Board Book Service, 1996.

Simme, Lois, *Auntie's Knitting a Baby, "Careful Connie",* Perfection Learning Corporation, 1985.

Stampler, Judith Bauer, *Wake Up Scooterville,* Scholastic Inc., 1994.

Wake Up Sleeping Beauty: A Pop-Up Book With Sounds, Dial Books for Young Readers, 1997.

Other Sound Books

Anastasio, Dina, et al, *Who's in the Shell (A Squeaky Surprise),* Reader's Digest Children's Publishing, Inc., 1996.

Aylesworth, Jim, *The Gingerbread Man,* Scholastic Inc., 1998.

Beylon, Cathy (Illustrator), *Mrs. Hen's Secret! (Squeaky Surprise),* Reader's Digest Children's Publishing, Inc., 1996.

Boynton, Sandra, *Moo, Baa, La La La*, Simon & Schuster Children's Books, 1982.

Bridwell, Norman, *Clifford Barks!,* Scholastic, 1996.

Carle, Eric, *The Very Quiet Cricket*, Putnum Publishing, 1990.

Cowley, Joy, *Tittle-Tattle Goose*, Wright Group Publishing, Inc., 1998.

Garcia, Emma, *Toot Toot Beep Beep*, Boxer Books, 2008.

Hewitt, Sally, *Squeak and Roar (Get Set...Go!)*, Children's Press, 1994.

Hood, Susan, *Max's Train Ride: A Squeaky Storybook About a Very Special Day!*, Fisher Price Staff/Thompson Bros. Staff, 1997.

Hood, Susan, et al, *Squeaky Shape Playbooks*, Reader's Digest Children's Publishing, Inc. 1997.

Mayer, Andy, et al, *Fire Trucks (Look & Listen/Board Book)*, Scholastic Inc., 1993.

Schertle, Alice, *Little Blue Truck Leads the Way*, HMH Books for Young Readers, 2009.

Weiner, Marcella et al, *I Want Your Moo: A Story for Children about Self Esteem,* Magination Press, 2009.

Games

Blow the Cotton Ball Race using a straw
Duck, Duck, Goose Game
Go Fish, School Zone, 1999.
Hedbanz, Spinmaster, 2010.
Imagine That Animal Lotto, African Safari Edition, DaMert Company, Berkeley, California, 1996.
Kids on Stage, University Games, San Francisco, California, 2015.
Language Arts Trivial Pursuit, by Mary J. Cera, Good Apple, 1992. (Available through Kino Learning Center).
Spot It Junior Animals, Blue Orange Editions, San Francisco, California, 2010-2014.
Songs We Sing, Frank Shaffer/ Carson Dellosa Publishing Co., Greensboro, North Carolina, 1976.

Equipment

Computer with microphone
Karaoke machine
Puppet Theatre
Puppets
Voice Recorder
Toy megaphone with voice enhancer
Two small message recorders

Internet Sites

About Health
> **World Wide Web**
> URL:http://socialanxietydisorder.about.com/od/otheranxietydisorders/a/
> **selectivemutism.htm**

American Speech, Language and Hearing Association (ASHA)
> **World Wide Web**
> URL: http://www.asha.org

The National Center for Biotechnology Information
> **World Wide Web**
> URL: http://www.ncbi.nlm.nih.gov/pmc/articles/PMC2925839/

The Selective Mutism Foundation
> **World Wide Web**
> URL: http://selectivemutismfoundation.org

The Selective Mutism Group/Childhood Anxiety Network
> **World Wide Web**
> URL: http://selectivemutism.org

The Silence Within
> **World Wide Web:**
> URL: http://www.selective-mutism.com

Yahoo Selective Mutism Support Group
> **World Wide Web**
> URL: https://groups.yahoo.com/neo/groups/Selectivemutismsupportgroup/info

Software

Wiggle Works, Scholastic Inc., 2004.

Any Phonics program to encourage the production of letter sounds such as **Reader Rabbit** or **Jump Start.**

Any game simulations to use as rewards.

Songs

"Baby Bumblebee", Road Trip Sing-Along CD, Mood Media Entertainment, 2012.

"How Much is that Doggie in the Window?", It's Party Time, K-Tel, Golden Valley, Minnesota, 1997.

Music That Teaches CD, Zoo-Phonics Products, Groveland, California, 1997-2010.

"Old MacDonald", Animal Songs and Stories, Rock Me Baby Records, 2012.

"Over in the Meadow", Animal Songs and Stories, Rock Me Baby Records, 2012.

"The Wheels on the Bus", Toddle Favorites, Music for Little People, 1998.

Any songs that would include sounds

Many song lyrics with animal sounds may be found at www.kididdles.com

Appendices

Name_____
Goals for Communication
September

Practice verbalizing three times a week by recording on the computer using Scholastic, Wiggle Works computer Program. Listen with a partner and/or teacher.
　　Dates_____

Record stories at school or at home to be played as part of a classroom theme study and center.
　　Dates_____

Make animal sounds.
　　Dates_____

Play board games using two voice messengers to answer Yes and No questions.
　　Dates_____

Mouth "Yes" and "No" to answer board game questions.
　　Dates_____

Us puppets to make animal sounds.
　　Datcs_____

Record a speaking prompt to be played in the regular classroom.
　　Dates_____

Record with a friend in the room.
　　Dates_____

Record with the teacher outside the slightly open door.
　　Dates_____

Whisper "Yes" and "No" to answer board game questions.
　　Dates_____

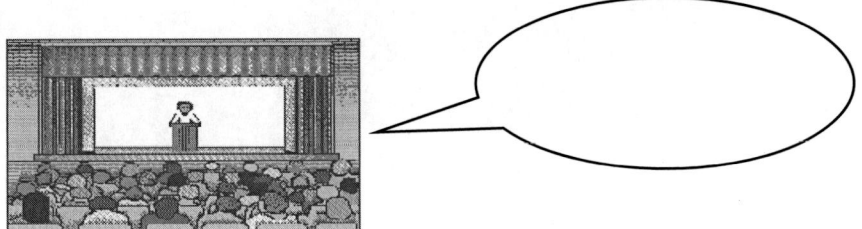

Class #1:

Class #2:

Class #3:

My Goal for September_____

Monetary Incentive Chart

5 Cents	
10 Cents	
20 Cents	
25 Cents	
50 Cents	
$1.00	

Prize #1

Prize #2

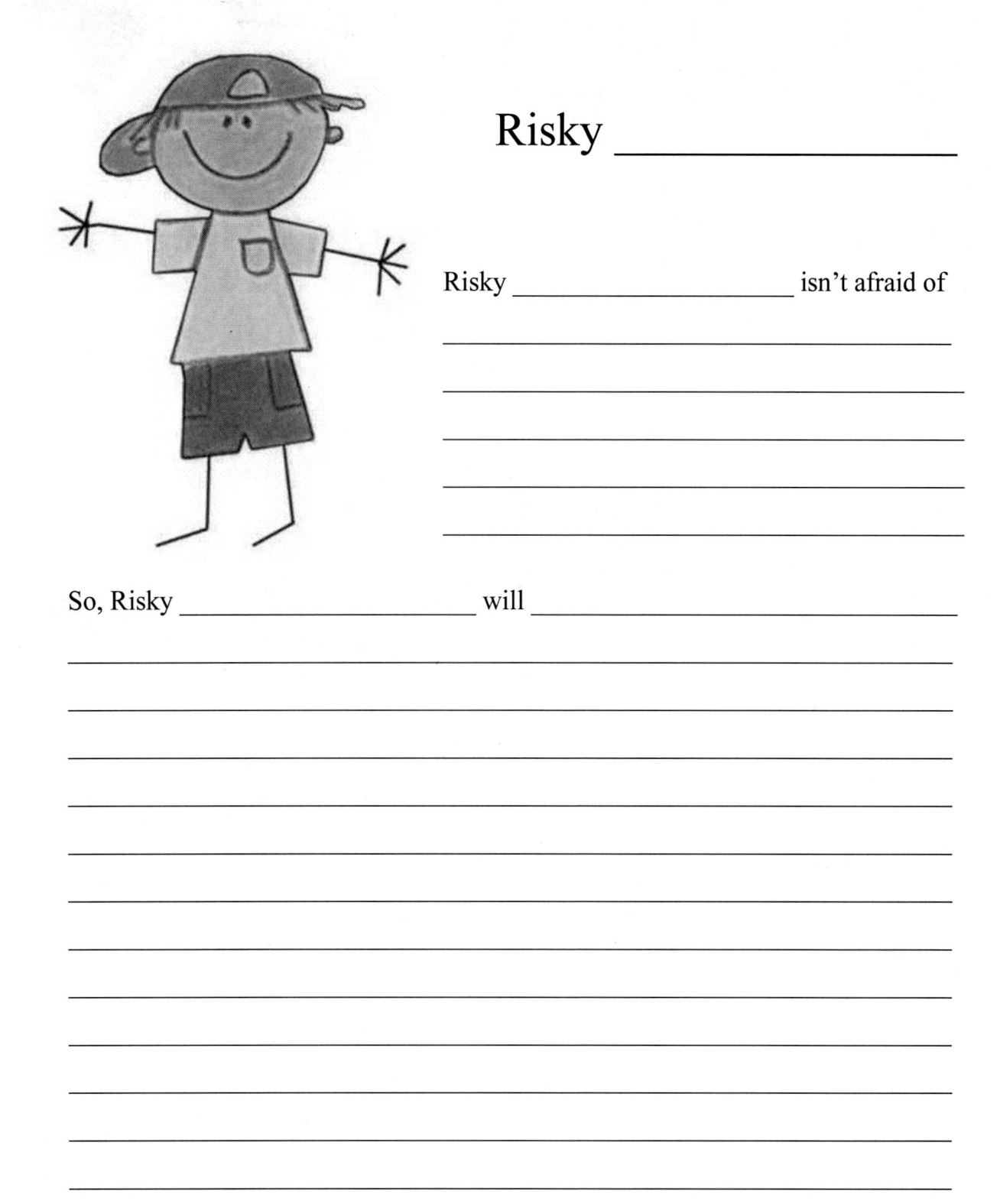

Risky _____

Risky _____ isn't afraid of

_____

_____

_____

_____

_____

So, Risky _____ will _____